Dedicated to my loving and inspirational grandmother Lupe Chipolina (Mama), the 'Rock' of our family.

When she heard about my accident, she dropped everything and flew from her home in Gibraltar to England, providing unwavering support to myself and my mum. She encouraged me to tell my story as she believed it would be a source of encouragement and inspiration to others.

Thank you, Mama, for everything.

I must thank my parents and my brother for all their love, support and sacrifice. Throughout the years, especially after my accident, their dedication, continued belief, and encouragement has gotten me to where I am today. Their help meant I felt content and confident enough to share my personal experiences about my journey with traumatic brain injury.

Special thanks must be given to Patricia and Taz, who spent countless hours transcribing my dictation, never becoming fed up or annoyed.

None of this would have been possible without the help of my talented cousin, who used her knowledge and expertise to help with formatting my story so I could share it with others who find themselves in a similar situation.

Thank you to my closest and dearest friends who have remained a great source of support, maintaining communication and even including me on their milestone occasions and significant life events.

My final dedication is to my Nanny Win. My accident had a positive impact on our relationship. She understood different situations I would experience in my recovery as she had personally experienced these with my grandad after his stroke. She gave me such helpful advice and unrelenting support that I will be forever grateful for.

Contents

One

Where It All Began

I was born on the 27th of July 1989 in Harlow to a married, loving mother and father. I have a brother who is 17 months older than me. We moved to Enfield, where we lived until my first year of secondary school, after which we moved to Shoeburyness in Essex. I completed my GCSEs and then went on to Southend Essex college to study BND public services to become a police officer in the army. However, I changed my career goals, leading me to Bristol. I attended UWE, the University of West England in Bristol, to study business and accounts. I was there for four years and held numerous part-time jobs to help fund my time there. I also had summer jobs back home. I graduated with a 2.1, then moved to a small village in Oxford with my boyfriend.

I found a job in the next town for an American company accounting for all their international trades. I spent many days after work in the village pub where I met up with my boyfriend and friends. I would play pool and darts whilst enjoying a few ciders. It was a short walk from my flat, above the village petrol station.

The 25th of May 2014 was a bank holiday, which started like any other day. I went to the pub with my friends and my boyfriend Neil. We stayed there for a while and then decided to take it up a gear, as we all had the day off. We went to the Crazy Bear Hotel for some cocktails. Half of us were outside in the smoking area, and the other half remained inside. I then went missing, to what I can only imagine was to use the toilet in my flat, which was next to the hotel. I did this regularly when out drinking as I had an uncommon phobia of public toilets. A young glass collector was attending the rooms when he noticed me. Neil then received a call from the Crazy Bear Hotel. They told him I had been found at the bottom of the stairs leading up to our flat. I was unresponsive, and an ambulance had been called.He rushed back to the flat to find me lifeless on the floor, with blood all over the wall and stairs. He put his jumper under my head whilst waiting for the ambulance to arrive. When the paramedics arrived, I had to be intubated at the scene. I had an endotracheal tube through the mouth and into the airway, so I could be put on life support. I was then rushed to John Radcliff Hospital in Oxford, where I underwent life-saving brain surgery.

I had a massive part of my skull removed to allow space for the swelling in my brain. During surgery, I suffered multiple strokes, which caused the left side of my body to be paralysed. I was fitted with a shunt to help drain the excess fluid on my brain. The shunt is a small tube that leads from my brain, around my ear, through my chest cavity, to my stomach lining. This allowed my body to re-absorb the fluid through my stomach.

I remained in a coma on life support for several months

with my parents travelling daily to Oxford. I experienced brainstorming on many occasions. Brainstorming or Symptomatic storming happens after someone has a Traumatic Brain Injury or is in a coma. Brainstorming causes your body to go into overdrive. Your heart rate races to a dangerous rate, and you begin to sweat profusely to the point where it looks like someone has poured a bucket of water over you. I was then transferred to Southend hospital and placed in a high dependency ward until I went to Northwick Park Hospital in Harrow on the 9th of September 2014, where I underwent assessments. It was there my Dad discovered that I could write. We were in the hospital's Costa Coffee, where I played with his phone. He asked if I thought I could write, I then proceeded to write the word

home

on an old receipt with my mum's pen, and just like that, the rest was history.

My mum then regularly bought writing pads and pens for me. From RRU, the people in charge of my funding decided to move me to a neurological rehab centre in Harlow. Where I had 3 weekly physio and speech and language therapy.

I now reside in a nursing home in Southend, so I am closer to my parents. I received 1-1 care 8 hours a day to enable me to carry out my day-to-day activities. This has helped me improve my speech and writing, and I am now on my way to reading again.

Two

Pictures Speak A Thousand Words

Me in 2011. I had the selfie bug.

My Aussie Sheila and I in 2012 at the pond in Stadhampton

First year at Bristol University.

We were never mature.

When my friend Jade and I hit the Big Apple in 2009.

Jade and I at the Rockerfella Centre

Me visiting my family in Gibraltar

Strike a pose!

A collection of pictures of Neil and I from 2013

The selfie bug continues...Me in 2013

Jade and I in 2007

I was the first member of my family to graduate from University in August 2010

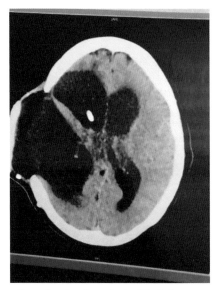

Scan showing the extent of the injury on my brain. The black shadow is the brain damage and the white spot is my shunt.

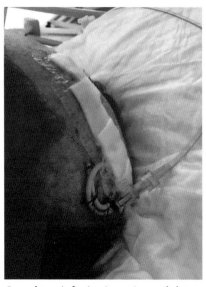

I caught an infection in my internal shunt, which had to be removed and replaced wth a new one

Two of my oldest school friends still take the time to come and visit me

Jade's wedding in 2019. She organised a ramp for my wheelchair to make sure I could attend

Three

Visualisation

Before my brain injury, I was very much into photography. When I visited home from uni, I always stole my dad's SLR camera. I took many scenic photos whilst taking our dogs for a walk along the seafront and while on holiday. I was well-known for always having my digital camera in my bag. Every night out resulted in taking hundreds of photos and videos (it made for some excellent hangover cures, to sit and look at all the pictures from the night before). I would then create albums and post them all on Facebook. My external hard drive is full of memories from school to the present. I was that annoying person who got pictures and videos of everything and everyone. I printed my favourites, and I covered my bedroom wall from floor to ceiling with memories at uni.

In Autumn 2014, after emerging from my coma, my cousin from Gibraltar was in London with her husband. They had been in and out of the hospital themselves with various appointments. My cousin Melanie had created a wall poster full of small pictures. She had hoped it would spark old memories and that the colours would enable me to focus. I have memories of spending countless hours staring at every picture. My mum even put everybody's names on the poster so the staff could talk to me about them. I put it up in every room I have lived in since receiving it.

 I love it as much today as when I first got it. I would like to create a new one with pictures taken since my brain injury. This will remind me that life does go on, albeit differently from what I expected. But it is still full of laughter and love.

Four

Friends Are The Family We Choose Ourselves

Part 1

After my accident, it showed me who my true friends were. One friend, in particular, has been my best friend since year 7 (first year of secondary school). We shared every major event! Even sharing our 18th Birthday party! We were in many of the same classes in school, sharing the same group of friends. We had many school trips together. We went skiing in Austria and to Disneyland in France. We also shared many holidays during the school breaks. We went to Menorca to her Nan's villa; she came to Gibraltar with me to see my family.

She went on to work for a Humanitarian Charity, so she was deployed abroad a few times. She kept in regular contact when she had access to the internet. She even visited me from the airport when she returned to the UK. I still say, 'she is the sister I never had,' and her family are like my second family.

Our joint 18th birthday party

Our typical Friendship photo- Sums up our personalities Perfectly

Dont Take
Life So Seriously

Living Our Best Life on holiday in Menorca.

The Water Could Have Been Warmer

She even made her sister go to Starbucks Drivethrough to get my favourite Frapaccino.

That's what I call extra special delivery!

Alice, Claire, Myself and Rachel.

The original Shoebury Girls

My friend Claire also joined us on school skiing trips. She involved me in her third pregnancy journey, giving me regular updates on her progress. I even suggested countless baby names, one of which was already a potential candidate. Claire even made a special effort to surprise me with a visit with her baby, just to meet them unofficially, but due to Covid, I had a surprise window visit instead.

It made my day!

Rachel's job took her to Australia, she did stay in contact, and although it may have taken a long time, she always made an effort to reply and visit when in the UK.

We are still close
friends to this day

Friends Are The Family We Choose Ourselves

Part 2

In secondary school, I became best friends with two extraordinary boys, who became close enough to be considered brothers. Luke was also in many of the same classes, so inevitably, I shared the same friendship circle. He went to university in York. Nick and I visited in his halls, which were so cold you could see your own breathing. I brought him an electric heater, which came in handy for our stay.

The boys came to Bristol on several occasions, and we continued our wild and reckless behaviour.

When I first had my accident, my mum was very good at informing them of my progress. They visited me in several hospitals, where they took the time to talk to me before I could interact properly.

The boys also went on numerous trips, including skiing and Menorca.

These boys have stood beside me through my darkest times and been a part of some happiest memories.

Later down the line, when I was in Sawbridgeworth, they even took the time to come just for the Manchester derby football match, where I wanted to write throughout. They took their time to learn how to understand my handwriting and have never got frustrated or annoyed at me. When I message, they always message back, making me feel involved with their life journeys.

I don't know what I
would do without them.

Friends Are The Family We Choose Ourselves

Part 3

Upon moving to Bristol, I moved into a shared flat of 6 mixed sexes. We fast became close, like a little family. One of my flatmates, Anna, became like my sister. One day I went to the student union shop and bought her a card because she was feeling a little bit down; little did I know that it said,

You make my fanny feel funny

After that, we had a new nickname, "fanny lover," for each other. It became interesting when my Mum or support worker had to write her a message with fanny lover. After my fall, Anna was brilliant at always replying to my messages and took the time to visit me regularly. We even went to the Cliffs Pavilion several times.

Although we didn't remain living with each other, we stayed close friends and ended up in the same nightclub almost every time we went out. Although we are no longer a couple of rooms away, I never felt distanced and trusted that she would continue to involve me in her life journey as she has so far.

Jade was introduced to me by my flatmate. We instantly hit it off as her course had some of the same subject units as mine. I also went to her house for New Year's Eve as my family lived in Gibraltar then, and I didn't want to spend it alone. Jade and I shared a common love of shopping. This led us to plan the best five-day holiday to New York City, retail therapy to the maximum. We had a full itinerary planned out for our entire trip, from places we would visit specific shops & restaurants, and we even pre-booked a helicopter tour over the city at night. needless to say, our suitcase was filled to the brim on our return with all the purchases and photos. Jade was lovely enough to choose her wedding venue so that I could attend in my wheelchair, rented a ramp and reserved seating inside the church for me and my parents. I gave her husband the nickname McFly because he looked like the lead singer of McFly. Jade recorded and sent me a video to announce her first pregnancy, and I would be anw auntie, which was terrific. I named her baby "Bubba McFly." She has kept me up to date with the progress of her pregnancy, making me feel involved. It is extra special of her to share such an intimate and personal experience as I will never get to experience it myself personally.

Thank you

from Mr & Mrs Sawyers

I can't wait to get my picture with Bubba McFly.

Another great friend I made was my beautiful Claudia. I met her as a student warden in the campus uni accommodation. Since my accident, Claudia has posted me postcards and fridge magnets whenever she has a trip to add to my collection. Claudia even made me 2 face masks which were more comfortable than those supplied by my care home.

I also had the pleasure of meeting my hippie, free spirit, Adi. She maintained regular contact, keeping me up to date with her worldwide travel adventures. We share a great love of music, taking us to many different events in Bristol. Our shared love of shopping gave us many hours of enjoying Bristol shopping and coffee.

Five

Self - Actualisation

I can't tell the exact time I had my accident, but I have vivid memories of the time I found out. It was in Northwick Park Hospital. My mum visited me as usual. She was stroking my hair as I looked around the hospital room. I wondered how I got there and where 'there' actually was. The most obvious question was 'how?'. WTF had happened? I heard nurses discussing me, so I had a rough understanding that I had fallen but had no memory of the events that had led to the accident. My last clear memory was in the pub.

My mum asked me if I understood what had happened, to which I indicated 'yes'. Mum then proceeded to explain all of the details that she knew. Although I understood what she was saying, I felt she was reading me a story from a magazine. I could not comprehend that the person she was talking about was me. It was not until I was in a wheelchair and first saw myself in a full-length mirror with a shaved head and some sort of plastic contraption on my neck that reality hit me hard in the face.

My lovely long hair had to be shaven so that the Doctors had access to my head for a life-saving operation. The plastic thing was a tracheostomy, which helped me to breathe unassisted. I hated to see how different the strokes had made my face look. It had fallen, making me look permanently angry. No matter how hard I tried to smile, my mouth would not lift.

I had become so accustomed to not eating or drinking that I overindulged when I was finally allowed. Food became one of the only things that I got to enjoy. Sadly, this saw me ballooning into double my initially small frame. I never thought being a classic 'big girl was a problem. However, I never was used to seeing the reflection of a completely different person. My weight then began to fluctuate. My mum was very lucky as being a Skinny Minnie meant all my lovely and expensive branded shirts went to her wardrobe. I gave my clothes to a young, thin girl who would enjoy them just as much as I did, and the rest of my clothes were given to charity.

I went through a phase of pure guilt; I felt guilty because of my parents' sacrifices due to my accident. I often lay in my bed alone, thinking it would have been better/more straightforward if I'd not survived. I asked Mum why she didn't choose to turn off my life support, and her response was first that they were never asked to make that decision and that my body was not ready to give up. I had fought this far.

If I were not meant to be alive, then I wouldn't be.

I still felt the same way in Sawbridgeworth, so I asked the house manager for a DNR. This made my mum so unhappy that I got it removed. These feelings got worse to the stage of feeling suicidal. I had figured out how easy it would be to drive my chair off the curb and into the road. I started to tell my mum & 1-to-1 that I wanted to go to Switzerland, where assisted suicide is legal. I felt as if my life was already over. My accident cost me so much. I struggled to focus on the positives in my life and what I could work towards. At this point, I received my first bit of counselling since my accident. Only 8 sessions of 1 hour focused mainly on accepting my accident, so they had minimal impact.

I usually tell my mum everything, but it was, and still is, very difficult regarding how I feel. She can't fully understand how I am feeling or why I feel that way because she has never been in that position. I try to hide much of what I feel because I know it would upset my mum to hear/see me in so much pain.

I have come to the stage in my life where all of my friends are buying houses, getting married and having kids. I have come to terms with the fact that I will never do the big 3. I feel guilty that my parents will miss out on being grandparents. I know they would make the best grandparents offering unconditional love, as they have done so for my brother and me. I am glad I have gotten to experience all of the good bits with my friends. I don't have to deal with the extra stress of baby weight.

So, in summary, although I lost my life as it was, I am truly blessed with the family and friends that I have to support me and share my life as it is now. I can share all of the milestones that I stand to miss out on.

Six

Hungry Hippo

After my initial accident, I was fitted with a feeding tube and later had a peg line inserted. I was peg-fed overnight and also had my medication flushed through my peg. If my medication was not already in liquid form, the tablets were crushed down to powder so they could be dissolved into the water flush. It may seem bizarre, but although the peg line was fed directly into the stomach, I could still taste what was passed through it. The peg feed left me with a sour taste. I was told this could have been from an acid reflux reaction, where I would have had the slightest bit of feed come back into my mouth, so I would have tasted it for real.

Although I was peg fed, I was still made to sit with others during mealtimes, which I remember as pure torture. I hated having to sit hopelessly watching people tuck into food. I was made to endure the smells. I had to listen to the sounds of cutlery and people chewing. I could remember the taste of many of the things I saw, and this alone would cause my mouth to fill with saliva. My poor parents would choose not to eat in front of me, as they knew the level of frustration and uncomfortableness I felt. If they were hungry, they would go so far as to ask my permission to eat in front of me. It felt nice that they had taken my feelings into consideration. Still, I would never have said no, unless it was something hot and smelly. I would ask if they minded doing it not directly next to me.

I was undergoing icing therapy to stimulate my lips and tongue to help encourage me to start using my voice or at least make noise again. The icing therapy involved using a spoon from the freezer to press against my lips and tongue. The temperature change meant increasing blood flow to the relevant areas to enable me to speak or make a sound.
During this time, my parents regularly took me to the hospital cafe, or my dad's favourite, Costa Coffee. We were slightly naughty as my dad used to give me the foam from the top of his coffee. This made my mum really concerned and worried about the possibility of choking (which never happened). I loved the taste of the creamy foam, and it really helped stimulate the movement of my tongue. Speech and language therapy then started. I began undertaking trials, some more successful than others. I could never stand the dull taste of water, even before my accident. When they started trying to give me water, it was no surprise I would refuse to cooperate. The water was also thickened.

The thickener not only made it the same consistency as wallpaper paste but also had a vile gritty texture. There was no way I would willingly eat the thickened water. This then progressed to yoghurt. I started on 10 teaspoons per day. My Auntie organised a party for my birthday where she bought every mousse flavour. It made me feel normal again to be included in the numbers because I was able to have one too.

The next stage was pureed food. It was nice to get the taste of food again; however, every meal looked precisely the same, a greeny brown colour with some bland mash. I was not able to know what it was that I was actually eating. The puree meals were fantastically presented when I was in Addenbrooke's Hospital. They used food moulds, making the puree look like actual food. My mum invested in a Ninja Bullet to puree my food herself. Mum then bought food trays with multiple compartments. Mum would look up different puree dishes three nights a week, then make and freeze them. My freezer in the care home was full of mum's cooking. I took one out every morning. This soon became mashable food, whereby I became able to eat anything that you could mash with a fork.

I did find that my brain injury had affected my taste and tolerance toward certain foods. I had an increased love for garlic and salt, but I still could not stand pork but found that I could now eat eggs without feeling ill. I still had my sweet tooth and love for barbeque sauce. My mum could not understand why I used barbeque sauce on everything until I made her try it herself. She now loves it and has stopped moaning at me.

When I proved to SLT that I was managing well with mashable food, they increased it to bite-sized pieces. I was able to eat my first KFC when the chef was ill. I used to say I deserved a treat. It was my first KFC in five years. How about that for a diet? It was my sin day.

I became accustomed to living off pizza from my uni days and being home alone, so this was a very big/proud day, the day I got to eat pizza. I have since had a Chinese and an Indian.

After several assessments, I could have my medication in tablet form with food. This meant that the only reason I still needed my peg was for flushes, as I could not consume enough to sustain myself. I am concentrating on increasing my daily fluid intake with the end goal of having my peg removed.

This is proving to be a massive struggle. Even before my accident, I didn't drink a lot anyway. On many occasions, I would say to my boyfriend that this was my first drink of the day. Coincidentally this happened to be in the pub with a pint, but seeing as cider is mainly either apple or pear, I argued that it was one of my five a day!

I used swabs to remove any remaining food in or around my mouth as I could not clear it myself. Swabs also helped remove the thickener coating that would remain after drinking. I have to purchase these swabs myself.

Seven

Finding My Voice

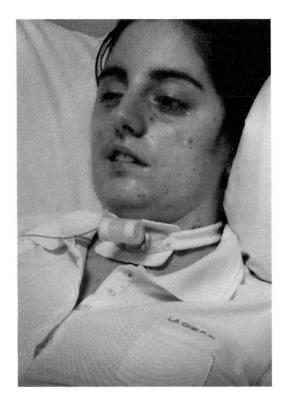

Doctors told my parents that the voice is always the last thing to be restored after suffering a brain injury. They also said to them that I would have my trachea indefinitely.

However, I am a Reeve;

Never underestimate the power and determination of a Reeve.

As I grew stronger, the trachea balloon was deflated slowly to allow more breathing air to enter my windpipe.

I defied the medical team and had it removed in 2015. Sadly, it healed wrong, leaving me with a pin-sized hole. When I coughed, phlegm would come out of the hole, which was off-putting to see but caused no pain or discomfort. I had to cross 2 plasters over the hole in my neck. This helped when in the shower or even when I had a bed wash. This prevented water from running into the hole, giving me the sensation of drowning, which would obviously scare me and cause me to panic. I had surgeries to open up the initial site and remove the scar tissue. This had to be done twice; the first time, it got infected and began to split.

I found it best to lay flat as it opened up my chest/airway, stretching my diaphragm so I could make noises & eventually speak. My first word was the classic 'no'. One day, I was getting personal care, and I began to count when I was laid on my side. My carer Pia then encouraged me not to stop. When I reached 100, I swapped to reciting the alphabet.

Considering doctors said I would probably never talk again, I amazed myself at how much I had achieved. My determination has beaten all the odds. I am a living medical miracle and proof that there is light at the end of the tunnel with love, support, and bloody hard work.

I went on to combine my physiotherapy with my speech and language therapy. When I was using the tilt table, I was flat, maximising productivity. My carer Lauren would regularly record videos for my mum and voice notes just to record my improvement. I made my mum swap to iPhone for the sole purpose of FaceTiming. This was also another way to communicate with friends and my family in Gibraltar. I would get mum to repeat what she thought I was saying so that I knew that she understood; if not, I would repeat it before writing what I was trying to say. I generally don't like talking to new people as I know that my speech is not always clear, so I try to avoid frustration for both myself and the new person.

I would love to meet the doctor who said that I would always have my tracheostomy tube and also that I would never speak again. I have a few choice, colourful words that I would love to say as long as my grandmother couldn't hear. I find it bizarre that all swear words are so easy to pronounce. It also amazes me that even with the amount of brain damage I sustained, I can still retain the knowledge of 2 different languages. One is French from school, and the other is Spanish from childhood, as my mother's side of the family are Gibraltarians. I regularly maintain contact via FaceBook, Facetime, Whatsapp and Instagram.

My family can usually understand what I am trying to say. At times will rely on my 1-to-1 carer to interpret what I write, especially when I am tired.

Pia helped me get my voice back. I really missed telling my family and friends that I love them.

Lauren became my friend and would regularly visit me in my care home.

Eight

Adapting Aspirations

Since my accident, I have had to change my life goals, but my main goal remains the same; living in my own house. The only difference is that it has to be adapted for my wheelchair. I have been told I might be better suited with a live-in carer, but I have not yet looked further into this possibility.

I think I'd better start playing the euro-millions!

I have already over-achieved in my education, going from school to college and, unexpectedly, to university. I ended up with a great local job. I was living with my boyfriend, who obviously became my best friend. We were in no rush to have a family or get married. Like many of our friends, we were happy enough to concentrate on working, regularly having lovely holidays, and not having to struggle with day-to-day living.

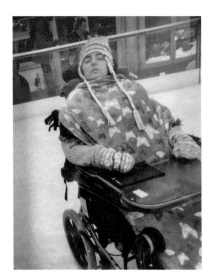

Since my fall, I have been ice skating as my manual chair went straight onto the ice rink.

My Grandad on my Dad's side had suffered a stroke, after which he used a wheelchair. He still managed to fly to Canada, so I knew I did not have to rule out going on holiday again. With excellent planning and support from my family, I flew to Gibraltar for one week on two separate occasions. I even celebrated my 30th birthday with my family in Gibraltar. The airline allowed me to travel in my wheelchair up to the plane, where I was transferred to a chair that would go down the aisles and then moved again to a window seat by an eagle hoist.

My Aunt and Uncle kindly went to stay at my Nan's, leaving their flat for my parents, me, my brother and a carer that came with us. I was made to feel normal when I got into the sea, and it was so bloody cold, a real shock to the system! It felt amazing not to have been left out. The beach in Gibraltar was the best-equipped beach I have ever seen. It had a gazebo to provide shade and privacy, an on-beach hoist & several different shaped buggies that could be submerged into the sea.

I have also been looking into brain injury support dogs. I think this would be very beneficial in several aspects of support; practical, emotional & psychological. My parents didn't believe such a thing existed when I first said I had found out about it. I regularly go to the cinema and play bingo. I was lucky enough to see Ed Sheeran at Wembley Stadium in 2018 with my mum. We had been many years ago to see Blue for mum's birthday. I also went to Colchester Zoo, where I fed a giraffe and an elephant. I can't believe how something as big as an elephant can be so gentle without being told by a trainer.

Nine

Music Is The Spice of Life

It has been widely documented that music can actually help in the recovery of brain trauma. Music has always been essential in my life; my parents had an extensive collection of vinyl, which I often referred to as 'big black CDs'. I would always play music at every opportunity. I had Hi-Fi in my bedroom and started with a portable Walkman before upgrading to a CD player. It was most strange if I was home for it to be silent, I would always fight with my brother over who rode shotgun in the car so that I could control the radio. I did have a vast selection of CDs, which I often used in my parents' car, much to their disgust. I eventually got a first-generation iPod Mini, in green, so I could store all my music in the same place. This was the same time that Limewire and Aries were popular download/file-sharing programmes. When this was full, I bought myself a silver iPod Nano.

I quickly became accustomed to having to have background noise to fall asleep. This saw my mum regularly coming into my room at night to turn off my TV. This continued until university when I often played music to fall asleep at night. During the day, I often had noise complaints from my neighbours.

It's uni student halls; why not live a little?

When I went on holiday, I always took an iPod docking station so that we had music when we were in the villa. I also used the iPod on the beach and around the pool.

Neil was a DJ in his spare time, so he always had the most recent and up-to-date music. When we were living together, our house always had some form of music playing. I regularly fell asleep whilst he was mixing, even though I was directly next to the speaker. Our neighbours began to hate us; however, I still argue that the music was never offensive. We never played it during unsociable hours or at an excessive volume. Neil bought me A new iPod Nano with more storage space and would regularly update it with the latest music.

After my accident, my parents bought me an iPod Shuffle so that I could listen to music. As I progressed, Neil regularly updated my iPod with new songs. I then started to compile lists of particular songs that I had heard on the radio that I wanted. Poor Neil would receive many lists, and some were not with complete details as I would often forget either the full song name or the artist's name. Still, he always managed to untangle the mess I would send over. In the new update, he would include these songs and others he knew I would like. In 2019, Neil bought me an iPod Touch that I would be able to operate myself. I still have the iPod Nano he bought me, and I use it daily. Eventually, I taught my mum how to upload music onto my laptop and then sync it to my iPod.

I still need music to fall asleep now, so I have learnt to play music at a reduced level to not disrupt other residents in the home. I play music on my iPod whenever I have personal care, including when I shower. I have become well known among the staff and residents for playing music. No matter how you're feeling at that particular moment, there is always music to match.

Music really
is the spice
of life.

Ten

Senior Moments

When I was a child, I always had great memories. I was constantly being asked to remember specific things to remind my forgetful mother.

In recent years, my mum and nan always blamed their age for forgetting things. The most common phrase was "it's just senior moment." After my accident, my long-term memories remained excellent, even recalling the names of people and places.

However, I found my short-term memory to be not as effective, and following the storyline in TV soap operas and dramas was difficult. Therefore, I gave up watching them daily. I only watched them when I was home more for my mum. I found the same with football, so I gave up trying to follow, just watching sports news for the results. My mum and I have a running joke of accusing the other of having one of their senior moments anytime something is forgotten.

I still remember films and the series Breaking Bad and Game of Thrones. I was following in the lead-up to having my accident. It's only within the last year that I have begun to watch the soaps and follow some Netflix series and British trash TV like Love Island... I absolutely love it.

Eleven

Back In The Day

As previously mentioned, I have a brother. He is 17-months older than me. We had the typical sibling relationship. We loved to hate each other, and as much as I disliked him at times, I would never stand for anyone saying a single bad word against him. Only I could do that. We always attended the same school.

When I was five years old, I suffered repeated ear infections, namely glue ear and tinnitus. I had 2 sets of grommets which resulted in severe scarring of my eardrum. This, in turn, led to hearing loss. I was issued with a hearing aid to help, which I used to hide by covering it with my hair. I remember the journey home and being surprised to hear my mum's leather jacket squeak properly for the first time. I had mastered the art of lip-reading. This made some people uncomfortable as I would look at their mouth movements as they spoke, but they thought I was rude and just staring at them.

I remember sitting up crying during the night, not wanting to go to school as I wasn't confident in learning the spelling set for homework. I couldn't break down the words. I literally had to memorise the spelling of particular terms. I remember learning to read with my nan. We used a Disney's Aladdin book, and I was made to read each paragraph repeatedly until I found a rhythm.

I was a bit of a goody-two-shoes at school, consistently achieving the highest grades on my school reports with the comments, "Laura is easily distracted." In year 9, I bunked my afternoon lessons for the first time and went to my friend's house and watched The Matrix Reloaded. I dropped myself in it with my parents when during a conversation, I said that I had seen the movie, so I had to admit how I had got to see the film as it was newly released...

Whoops!

My swimming ability went as far as knowing how not to drown, so I was enrolled in swimming lessons twice a week. I progressed through each ability group to eventually become a county swimmer. However, when it was suggested that I have a third practice before school, I quit altogether. This would have been too much to concentrate on at the same time as school. Also, the thought of getting up early for swimming before school was beyond realistically achievable. I did look into finding a swimming club when I moved to Shoeburyness but to no avail.

Whilst in secondary school, I was even given the unique opportunity to join the fire cadets. Every Friday, I, along with a small group of other teenagers, was taught all the fire brigade drills, even down to how to correctly use a fire extinguisher and blanket that you will find in most workplaces.

It was at the fire cadets that I first dislocated my thumb whilst using one of the old fashioned hoses. I could not control the level of pressure and it was too much, forcing my thumb to displace.

Whilst away skiing, I dislocated my thumb again, but it was not on the slopes; it was when we stopped for lunch. I slipped on the wet tiled floor in the toilet whilst wearing my chunky plastic ski boots; however, after it was put back into place and I had a cast fitted, I continued to ski. I was determined not to let this ruin my skiing trip.

I dislocated my weakened thumb for the third time, which was rather embarrassing, simply by falling off the end of my bed. This was not the last time. My dad was lovely enough to become my hairdresser, whilst I could not do it myself. Restricted by a cast, my dad even straightened my hair for me.

At the end of college in 2009, I went on another holiday to Menorca to my best friend's nan's villa. There were four of us, and it was a tranquil resort, a short bus ride from the capital city. It was here that we went on a glass-bottomed boat trip. However, I was terribly sick and subsequently "fed the fish." When we returned, we decided to go to the local English pub 'Kit Kat', where I met Neil with his friend. We spoke about Wimbledon and the Premier League transfer window. I threw caution to the wind, and when I met up later that evening with him, we exchanged numbers. It was the most embarrassing journey home from the airport with my parents as my friends enjoyed telling them I had met a boy on holiday. They described it as a 'holiday romance.' The following week, Neil came from Oxford to Shoeburyness to visit me; the rest was history. I went to Oxford near enough every weekend.

When I was 18, I managed to get a job at Harrods in Knightsbridge. One day I was approached by a woman who said I had lovely teeth. It turned out that she was from the marketing team for Colgate toothpaste. Later that month, I was picked up from Harrods in a limo and taken for a test shoot. They paid for me to have my hair cut & died to brunette. I was then offered a contract to go to Switzerland and do a Colgate advert campaign. However, this would have required me to leave university, and I did not think it was a long-term, solid investment of my time compared to the job I would get with my degree.

After completing my degree, I applied for a financial accountant position with BP based in New York City. However, I decided against it as I did not want to leave Neil or my family. It was not an option for Neil to move with me, so I declined the job offer. I instead moved to Oxford with Neil and started the job hunt again by signing with several agencies. I held several long-term positions before I found the financial accountant job in the next village, which was a short drive from the house. I was lucky enough to be insured to drive both my Fiat Punto and Neil's classic Mini. However, Neil's car was highly sought after by thieves. The first day I drove it to work, someone tried to steal the wheels. Having loosened the bolts, when I attempted to go home, the motion of speed bumps caused the wheel to fall off, causing me to make a very awkward and embarrassing phone call to Neil. I have never lived it down.

Neil and I never had the perfect relationship, but we always had fun and love. Neil supported me through all of my Melanoma appointments and treatments. When I had my accident, Neil maintained his support, regularly visiting me in hospital despite the long journey to the care homes, which were over 2 hours away from Oxford. He also keeps in contact via Whatsapp and video calls. He is a whizz at understanding both my writing and my speech.

Me throughout
the years

Turning down the BP position in New York turned out for the best. I would not have received the same level of medical care had my accident happened in the United States. Although I would have had medical insurance, I would have quickly exceeded the total amount that it covered.

My parents have always been my biggest supporters over the years and still remain the same today. I wouldn't be the person that I am today without them. My brother moved into his own flat nearby my current care home so I get to see him regularly.

I am very embarrassed at how terrible some of these photos are, however, they are relevant to my story and will at least give some people a giggle. I never want to talk about the state of my fringe. Yes, I know how bad it was, hence why I grew it out.

Little did anyone imagine what drama my future would hold...

Twelve

Communications

After emerging from my coma, my parents would time the number of seconds that I would keep my eyes open. I found it incredibly difficult to either focus on or track anything. The lights were on, but no one was home. This was the same time that my cousin had made me a wall poster of old family photos, with the hope that the colours would help me focus and that the photos would bring back memories. My mum went on to name every person that was in the images so that the staff could talk to me about them when she wasn't there. As previously mentioned, I spent hours staring at the posters on the wall and have put them up in every room, ward and space that I have been in since.

My mum attempted to help me track/focus by bounding around my bed. I would have loved to have heard what the staff who saw her must have said! I have vivid memories of my mum whispering in my ear that she was there, that I was ok and telling me that if I could hear her, to squeeze her hand. This gave me much comfort.

In the first attempts to get me to communicate, speech and language therapy used yes and no cards. I had to look up to answer 'yes' and down for 'no'. It is strange how quickly you run out of questions to ask that have yes or no answers. Although this was very helpful, it meant that I could not elaborate any further on my yes or no answer. I vividly remember opening my mouth, but no sound would come out. Inside, I was screaming. I would easily get frustrated with myself and the person that was trying to interact with me. It was in Northwick Park that I was first given a button that "spoke out" loud, saying 'It's Laura; I need some assistance, please." I couldn't bend my arm to reach the call bell, so I would sound the button, and if a member of staff was nearby, they would hear. Other people in the hospital bay would hear me pressing my button and would buzz their call bells on my behalf.

I was messing around with my dad's mobile phone in Costa Coffee. As I twizzled it in between my fingers, I realised it was like I was holding a pen. At this point, dad asked if I thought that I would be able to write. My mum sprung into action, grabbing a pen and an old receipt from her bag. I wrote the word 'home'. After that, my mum regularly bought writing pads and pens.

It was in Sawbridgeworth, where another resident's family suggested that I try to use a graphics tablet to write on. My mum now buys me LCD writing tablets, similar to the old school etch-a-sketch's. There I was, saving the rainforests.

As I began to find my voice, I used my writing board less frequently, only resorting to it as a backup for when I was tired or misunderstood. I still find talking to new people very embarrassing, and I tend to shy away and try to avoid awkwardness and frustration for myself and the person that I am with. I do have to remind myself that I have had several strokes. Therefore my speech will not be how it used to be before my accident. I have, however, improved remarkably! Especially considering that the doctor told me that I would probably never speak again.

I am most amazed that I can speak not only English but also French and Spanish. I have also been taught a few Italian words by the beautiful Italian carers working in Sawbridgeworth.

I have tried to use the eye gaze computer; however, I cannot focus for long enough to operate the software effectively. There must be other forms of technology available. Just look at what Stephen Hawking could do! I also was given Grid 3; however, it fast became impractical as it was too slow. In 2019 the nurse adapted the settings on my mobile phone, making the font size larger, which allowed me to type myself for the first time. It obviously helped that it had the predictive text. Still, I could send concise messages myself with hard work and persistence. I remember sending my mum a Whatsapp saying,

I love you.

I felt super proud that I could do it independently without relying on someone else. The same nurse also helped me discover that I could read, providing that it was extra large text. This helped restore some of the self-confidence that I had lost. I could not help but feel silly that I could not read, even though uni required me to read countless books. I felt slightly better about myself, knowing that I did still have that ability to read. Although, when it comes to smaller text, I do still need someone to help me out.

In my hospital bay in Northwich Park, there was a petite African lady named Joan Collins. She would always tell me who was in the bay and when I was in my wheelchair, if my head slumped, she would constantly say,

Lift your head up, Laura.

My dad would bring her a newspaper every time he came to the hospital to see me. She eventually went home, and we lost contact with her.

Back In The Day Continued...

My friends and I would regularly visit her parents and keep in contact with her sister. This was the first funeral outside of the family that I had ever attended. It was lovely to see the number of people that attended and to hear such kind, loving words about such a young, beautiful and promising young lady. I often reminisce about the great fun and memories we shared and wonder how different our lives would be now if that terrible accident hadn't occurred. We were both accident-prone. I had my first tattoo in dedication to Jo. I love looking at it because it obviously reminds me of her.

Around this time, James' Dad approached me with the offer to pay for me to attend uni out in America. James was from a financially privileged family, and his dad disapproved of my working-class background. I took great pleasure in telling his dad to poke his offer where the sun didn't shine.

I could make it by my own merit!
I did not need his handout.

James coincidentally ended up in the same uni as me, Bristol university, much to his dad's dislike. Devastatingly, James had a head-on collision a year to the day Jo had her fatal accident. Sadly, the decision was made to withdraw his life support due to the inactivity of his brain. His family helped with two funerals, one in England and one in America. I refused to attend either funeral as his dad had said that if I had accepted his offer, James would have followed me to America. He believed this meant he would never have had the accident. I cannot describe the level of guilt that this made me feel. I did keep in contact with his brother and sister for a short while after his death.

In 2012, my dad and I scoured the internet looking for puppies when we came across 'Bella'. Mum wasn't open to having a Staffie due to their reputation and associated horror stories. Still, dad and I had fallen in love and eventually won the 'fight of the puppy'. Mum and I were in the hospital waiting for me to have an operation as part of my treatment for melanoma. We sent countless name suggestions to my dad until we all decided on 'Bella', which was very fitting as she was bloody beautiful! Mum started taking her to work with her as it was too long for a puppy to be left alone. Every day, I would ask mum, 'do you love her yet?'. Bella quickly became mum's shadow, following her everywhere. I would regularly take both Jimmy and Bella on long walks. I even took them to Rossi's Ice Cream Parlour to get them their own tub of ice cream!

In my first year of uni, I suffered from episodes of blacking out. I was admitted to the hospital, and after investigation, it was discovered that I had a nodule on my brain. Stress would cause my ventricles to inflame, causing me to pass out. I could usually feel when this was about to happen. When I stupidly fell off my bed again, dislocating the dreaded thumb, Fanny Lover took me to the hospital. She stayed with me whilst it was put back into place, and I had my cast fitted. I did not let this stop me from enjoying nights out. I just made sure to match my outfits to the colour of the cast and that I was not bumped. It made nights out cheaper as alcohol had a more significant effect while taking painkillers. The moral of the story is I should not sit on the edge of beds, even if I am sober. It will always end in tears and a trip to A&E. I finally had a butterfly hinge screwed on to stabilise my left thumb so it wouldn't happen again.

Bella was extremely clever. Whenever I was at home or in the car, she would jump up on the sofa and sit by my side, resting her head on my lap so she didn't touch my bad arm. It was as though she could sense that something was wrong. It was bizarre but lovely.

Sadly, Jimmy developed several health issues as he grew older, and we lost him on the 11th of November, 2016, at 9 years old. He left a massive gap in the house, and Bella was left confused and missing him. One day, Bella was ill, so Mum took her to the vet. They decided on exploratory surgery as she was usually very fit and healthy. We had no explanation as to what was causing her to be so ill. Upon the surgery, lesions were found on her liver. Mum had to make the heartbreaking decision to let her go on the 2nd of April 2019. This obviously left our house completely dead, and mum had said that she would never have another dog.

However, at the end of April, Poppy came along. Even so, our house is nowhere near as happy as when we had two dogs. So, in my annoying ways, I have started telling my parents that Poppy needs a doggy friend, much to my mum's disgust. "I've heard it all before!" she proclaims. Watch this space. I might not live in the family home anymore. However, I'm still very much an active member of the family. I will voice my opinion whether they approve or not.

Thirteen

Humour

I am often told that I have a warped sense of humour. I use humour as a poor attempt to mask my insecurities. If I can get in there first and make a joke about my disability, I can avoid comments from others around me. I can also answer many questions that most people are afraid to ask. I feel that if I can make a joke, then it will make those around me feel as though I am more approachable.

I am not easily offended at all!

I tell my carers that when they leave my room at night, I jump out of bed, start Irish dancing, and say that one of the benefits of being disabled is that I always have a seat! It also gives me the advantage of not queueing up in many high street stores. I have the express lane to everything! I get free parking, discounts in the cinema and theatre, and even my Ed Sheeran concert tickets were 'specially packaged.'

I do wear slippers most of the time as they are more comfortable. Slippers save me time as I don't have to worry about what shoes match my outfit. However, I do have several pairs of sandals for when the weather is occasionally pleasant enough. I often say that I might well be severely disabled, but I'm severely disabled with a bloody degree. Let's not forget that.
I often use humour as a defence mechanism. Suppose I am the first to joke about the stuff I am most insecure and uncomfortable with. In that case, people won't bother to mention 'the elephant in the room'. I believe that people probably think it anyway but are just too polite or shy to mention or say anything.

I often hear people trying to whisper to each other when I am out in public. Usually, it is just people saying, "Ah, poor girl, I wonder what happened." I was not born this way. One time stands out particularly prominent as it was really hurtful. It was just after Jadey had told me that she was pregnant. Naturally, I started looking at newborn baby things. Suddenly, I overheard a woman say to her partner, "How is it possible that someone in her situation could ever have a baby? Wouldn't that be unfair on the baby?" I felt like screaming. I replied, "not that it's any of your bloody business, but I am looking for my friend that is having a baby! Not for me!".

I often swear because it is funny that the doctors said I would never speak again, but there are certain swear words I would never use in front of my mum out of respect. Whenever I make blunders, I often blame them on my brain injury. 'It's not my fault. I have a brain injury!' I use the 'disability card' to escape sticky situations.

I often told my mum that I wanted to make a sign that said, "Didn't your mum teach you not to stare? It's rude," so I could just hold it up when I was out. I joke that when I had my fall, God refused me. It wasn't my time. I still needed to cause more mayhem, so he sent me back.

My fall made me lose many aspects of my life. However, I have never lost my sense of humour! If I don't laugh, I'll cry!

I have never lost my sense
of humour!

If I don't laugh, I'll cry!

Fourteen

Cold Hands,
Warm Heart

My accident caused damage to the part of my brain that allows you to regulate/maintain your body temperature, 'the thermostat'. Therefore, I have to rely on my mum and my carers to guide me concerning my choice of clothing and whether I need to use a blanket! Before I went to Gibraltar, I had to acclimatise by using just a bed sheet and wearing short-sleeved t-shirts during the day. I also had to wear short-sleeved nighties for bed instead of my usual long sleeves.

Before my accident, I was forever cold. I never could stand fans. I always wore long-sleeved shirts, jumpers and scarves. I was always known for wearing hats. When I went to uni, I was called a 'granny' for having an electric blanket! It was here in Bristol that I started expanding my collection of blankets.

Every day I would curl up in a ball underneath my blankets for a 'power nap.' I would say that that was my Hispanic side needing a siesta.

It was in my blood.
I'm not being lazy!

When really, it was either that I was still recovering from the night before or preparing myself for more mayhem that night! Friends would come to my house and always steal my blankets.

I would always use a blanket when chilling out in the living room. This continued when I moved to Oxford. I would even use Neil as a human hot water bottle all night! I would even wear his socks after he had taken them off and they were still warm (if he didn't know then, he does now). However, as much as I hated feeling cold, I hated the feeling of my feet getting too hot, and I would kick them off after warming up.

When my fall, the hospital staff put a fan in my room. However, I obviously still had a hatred for fans, and my body would react, causing all of my machines to alarm, only to settle down when someone came in and turned the fan off. When I was Sawbridgeworth, I used to refuse to have the fan on unless it was pointed away from me; and only ever when carers were in my room. They had to turn it off before they left! The same as my window had to be open whenever my parents were due to visit.

I was always given extra blankets in the hospital when they opened the ward window. My mum would bring me my own blankets from home, and they were softer than the hospital ones, and they gave me comfort as they smelt of home.

When I moved to Shoebury, It all changed. I choose to always have my window open unless it's raining! I have a warm duvet cover for the nighttime. However, I have used only the top sheet and one blanket on my bed. I also have a fan for the carers to use, as long as it is not pointed directly at me. I also have a small, compact dehumidifier that doubles up as a fan.

I think it's safe to say that although I have a cold exterior, I have a very warm heart!

Fifteen

Accepting Change

I was always a very private and reserved person. I didn't even like to wear clothes that showed too much flesh. However, straight after my accident, I relied wholly on care staff for all aspects of my personal care. I could no longer do things for myself, which at times has left me feeling embarrassed, exposed and vulnerable.

I even rely on them for the simplest tasks, like scratching an itch on my face or back where I cannot reach myself. It is simple stuff that I used to take for granted. I remember feeling jealous of others who could do these things themselves. I used to think about how lovely it would be to just have a scratch without needing assistance. I would annoy staff by always calling them only because I had an itch.

After my fall, my womanly/monthly cycle stopped. Although I did not miss the pain and hassle connected to the menstrual cycle, it did leave me feeling like I was less of a woman. I became particularly emotional when close friends became pregnant, as I knew it would never be possible for me. This made me want to become very involved with my friends' pregnancies. I even joked with my best friend that when she has children, she'd better make me a Godmother as it would probably be the closest thing to being a mother that I would get!

Before my accident, my doctor told me that if I were to have a child, there would have been a 50% chance that I would pass on the mutated gene that carries my melanoma. At this point, I decided not to have children. I wouldn't feel comfortable knowing my baby would have a high chance of going through all that I had to endure because of my melanoma. Obviously, it has never stopped me from wondering "what if". I try to lighten the subject by saying that not having to deal with periods or children is one of the positive things I can take due to my accident.

My accident spurred me to re-evaluate some of those who I considered being close friends. I am aware that "life goes on." Regardless, I found it incredibly difficult to comprehend why some people would just not reply to me when I took the time and effort to contact them. I am still taken aback by the sheer level of support and contact that I have received from my family, especially my family in Gibraltar. Despite living in a different country and having their own families and careers, they always kept in regular contact.

My English family have also got their own family. They have demanding jobs but, again, always maintain regular contact and would visit me.

The decision was made to sell my car when it became clear I would never be in the position to ever use it again. Many of my sins became apparent when my parents picked up my car. They discovered many McDonald's wrappers from where I used to have a Friday McDonald's breakfast. Whoops! I didn't discard the evidence very well, if at all. It gave us all a giggle.

I became very annoyingly persistent when messaging my boyfriend or closest friends.

As I previously mentioned, I damaged the part of my brain which regulates my body temperature. I had to follow the advice and guidance given by others to ensure I would not overheat. However, my brain was telling me I was cold. My body would often be hot, so I would leave off my blanket and refrain from wearing too many layers or thick items.

My parents and brother showered me with unbelievable amounts of love and support. They allowed me to get to the stage of feeling comfortable and content with the person I am today with the very different life I need. My dad always said we must focus on making the best of life as it is now and not dwell on how life could or should have been. My parents have always been my rock. I will never be able to repay them for everything they have done.

I have always said I don't want to be treated any differently. I am still 'normal'. I might have a brain injury, but I still have all my marbles. Although, this is questionable as I was never conventionally normal to begin with.

We must focus on making the best of life as it is now and not dwell on how life could or should have been.

Sixteen

Addiction

I always had an addictive personality and quickly became obsessed and repetitive with everything. This later became apparent in my teenage years. I never really experimented with anything beyond cannabis. Despite many opportunities, I had seen the effects of other drugs. As a result, I was scared to even attempt to try anything. Weed was a plant, and it wasn't costly.

After my accident, I was in extremely high levels of constant pain, so I was given Oramorph (an oral version of morphine) regularly. This helped me maintain control over my pain level. However, it became apparent my body became addicted to the Oramorph and that it had become accustomed to it. Therefore, it stopped having the desired effect.

The team then decided to try me on Tramadol. At first, it again helped with my pain. But my body became intolerant to that as well. When I was having both Tramadol and Oramorph, it made me particularly sluggish and slow. As a result, I stopped trying to speak, and I found it very difficult to write. I regularly fell asleep. The drugs made me high and stopped my pain. I would forget about the pain only because I was so high.

Therefore, this only masked the pain and did not solve the problem.

At the same time, many reports were in the news about the long-lasting effects of Tramadol. Mum and I googled the effects of Tramadol, and she printed it for me and said I needed to stop taking it. I was tested on Codeine; however, it had no effect other than causing severe constipation, a common side effect of Codeine. Now, I alternate the simple Paracetamol and Ibuprofen throughout the day. I also have Amitriptyline in the evening, which acts as a sleeping aid, along with my Baclofen. Any pain level is manageable. I don't want to mess around too much while my pain is bearable. Considering the damage my accident caused, I know I will never be ultimately pain-free. However, I am happy with the pain being tolerable.

I would, however, advise anyone against using opiate-based pain relief due to how quickly you can become addicted to them. Clearly, they only mask the problem and do not solve the initial issue.

I often try to make fun of my meds by saying at least now my drugs are legal as they are prescribed by the Doctor. I also have the added bonus of my drugs being free as I don't pay for my prescriptions. It has taken me a long time to realise and accept that using any drug is not a very good or long-term solution.

Seventeen

Covid- 19

It was March 2020. I was in Addenbrookes hospital, where I had been admitted for investigations into possible complications with my shunt. Thankfully, all was deemed okay, with no further action needed. Upon returning, I was sad to learn that there was a national lockdown and the Covid-19 pandemic was declared.

I returned home to find that the care home was in total lockdown, and all residents had been isolated for a fortnight. Upon being released from isolation in our rooms, we were still confined to the care home and communal areas, maintaining social distancing. This proved challenging, particularly during lunch and dinner, with many residents being forced to change their everyday seating arrangements.

We were still allowed pre-booked, socially distanced, outside visits with one person, preferably the same person each week. This immediately caused problems as I had my parents and my brother to consider, which was obviously more than the one visitor I was allowed. I knew management was not in on the weekend, so I booked a visiting slot for this time. I was 'naughty' and would regularly exceed the number of visitors. I could not see the logic or the harm in seeing my parents simultaneously. We all wore face masks, and we were all outside!

My Grandmother from Gibraltar was in the UK, so she was essentially stuck due to the lockdown, preventing her from flying home to Gibraltar. Selfishly, I saw this as a silver lining as I loved having my nan up the road, and I was regularly spoiled with home-cooked meals

Just like Mama used to make.

We were only permitted to leave the care home for essential appointments like the dentist. This was nice because we could get out, but not exactly for what I would consider jolly or fun. The home then started to allow one regular visitor to enter, strictly confined to the meeting room, which was better than being outside due to the unstable and unreliable English weather.

As time rolled on, the lockdown ended, but nothing was relaxed in the rules for residents or the home. My mum took the opportunity to fly my nan (Mama) home. I was sad as this meant that Mama could no longer do window visits. I was most disappointed when I was denied permission to hug or kiss her goodbye! I felt this was not justified as she had been shielding throughout this Covid pandemic. When I said that I would willingly isolate, I was still denied!

I had a hairdresser's appointment scheduled for December, which I annoyingly had to cancel as I was not allowed to leave the care home. On Christmas Day, I was lucky enough to be able to book a slot for visitors. All gifts had to be quarantined and sanitised for 48 hours before we could open them. The weather stayed dry, but it was bitterly cold, so I wrapped up in blankets and wraps.

In summary, come the weekend, the managers were not on site to view the 'rule-breaking', and I was only 'bending' the rules. Other residents totally disregarded the rules, even when managers were in and were not reprimanded for their actions. This caused me massive anger and frustration. One resident was caught kissing her boyfriend, which infuriated me as I was desperate to kiss and hug my elderly grandmother goodbye. Still, I was denied (little did they know I had done it anyway! What's the worst that could have happened? It would have been worth the isolation!) I understand the concern regarding personal contact, as my care home managed to maintain the highest level of care throughout this pandemic and kept all residents safe. Not one person contracted Covid!

During the lockdown, I helped both parents celebrate their 60th birthdays. I even told a white lie to get my bank account details to buy presents, cards, and a birthday cake! We also had Mother's Day, and I created a beautiful hamper full of my mum's favourite chocolates (they didn't last long!) I also had my good friend make personalised Mother's Day cupcakes, which were beautiful to look at and tasty!

May 2021 was exciting as my cousin's wife gave birth to my extremely adorable little second cousin. I couldn't wait to meet him and have a squeeze! At this point, I had 3 little bubbas to meet. I had been planning my first outing for when the rules were finally lifted. I had an entire year of shopping, bingo and casinos to make up for. Ashford Retail Centre had better watch out!

Once Covid restrictions were updated on the Government guidance, we had to wait for the care home to accept and modify the advice in the guidelines. This was expected to take a couple of weeks. For example, after I attended a "routine" melanoma dermatology review concerning a suspicious mole, I was placed  into isolation. However, when the government guidelines changed to state that isolation was unnecessary if residents had routine hospital and doctor appointments, I was immediately released.

However, tomorrow I am undergoing a day procedure to remove my ingrown toenail. Still, because this is classified as day surgery, I have to follow the policy of technically being admitted to the hospital. Which entails; 3 days before isolation and a fortnight of isolation once it has been done. I hope the government updates the guidelines. Obviously, it would be 'low risk' as all hospital staff wear appropriate PPE, and it would be in a sterile environment.

Eighteen

Friends Are The Family We Choose Ourselves

Part 4

For as long as I can remember, I have been told that friends are the family we choose for ourselves. Treat others how you wish to be treated yourself. A true friend would be there for support in the darkest of times and be there to share the happiest times.

Mum is part of a group of 7 friends who remain close today. A few of them I refer to as 'Auntie.' I also became friendly with their children. One of mum's friends worked within the care sector and came to Gibraltar with us the second time to help my mum with my personal care. She has also provided mum and me with a lot of guidance with her knowledge of the care system. It has been most beneficial.

The first statement was made very accurate when I had my accident. My best friends were there for me, not only travelling to see me in multiple hospitals and several care homes. They've always been on the end of the phone, sending me messages and replying to mine. No matter where they were at the time, they always made a conscious effort to maintain contact. In particular, Alice, who has a humanitarian job, or 'saving the world as I like to call it. This had taken her to different continents and limited her access to the internet. When given opportunities, she even video-called me. When she's back in the UK, she always makes a concerted effort to visit me. Even coming straight from the airport once or twice, bringing my favourite Starbucks coffee.

I have been friends with Luke, Nick, and Alice since my first year of Secondary School. We all shared the weekend by visiting many local attractions such as the cinema, bowling, Lakeside and Bluewater shopping centres, and Peter Pans (Adventure Island). We regularly went to the swimming pool in Chelmsford, where they had a wave machine. As previously mentioned, we all went on several ski trips with the school and shared a holiday in Menorca. It was the first, along with many weekends, at my university in Bristol and Luke's university in York. Claire had been friends with the boys for many years prior.

Nick, Claire, Alice and I all had a birthday around the same time. This made it very easy to remember who had a birthday coming up. Nick, Alice, Claire and Luke were all a great form of support when we tragically lost our good friend Joanne. Claire introduced me to Rachel, who would end up working in Australia. Again Rachel, like Alice, would maintain regular contact with me by messages. They both made a special effort to visit me in my care homes when in the UK. They all know everything there is to know about me. My uni friend, originally from the Cayman Islands, would regularly message me from her home abroad or in London.

Through the power of social media, Facebook and Instagram, I have been able to stay in contact with friends-dating as far back as Primary School. It proved to be a daunting and somewhat difficult time when I had to answer the common question of 'what have you been up to lately?' I had to explain in summary my fall and the impact it has had on my life.

Never in my wildest dreams could I imagine someone close to me having an accident that ended with them in a wheelchair, let alone it happening to me!

At uni, I formed a sisterly relationship with both Anna and Jade. Our friendship is proving to stand the test of time. They are still not only around but also visit regularly and maintain constant contact through messaging and social media.

My accident left me emotionally fragile. This caused me to feel very confused and somewhat hurt as I had many people that I would have called my' friends' in Oxford that, after my accident, appeared to have dropped off the radar. Many would not respond to my messages, but I understand that life continues for everyone around me. However, I cannot comprehend why someone would read my message and not reply. This did have a significant impact on my self-esteem to begin with. However, now I have adopted the attitude of 'I'm not going to waste my time chasing you.' They're not bothered or as good a friend as I thought. So whatever, get on with it! I don't expect or want sympathy. I actually find it rather condescending and sarcastic when sympathy is shown.

Since living in care homes and interacting with many different staff members, I quickly became friendly with specific individuals despite being considerably older than them. I had many common interests, such as; music, fashion and celebrity gossip, and I built a good and strong professional relationship with the care staff through these similarities. I can give advice/ my opinion on many scenarios which I have personally experienced.

My accident has a silver lining... all the people I have met and other residents have been fascinating, and it is nice to have formed connections/ bonds with them. In Sawbridgeworth, I found great comfort in recognising 2 of the residents and their families from my time at Northwick Park. It was a bizarre coincidence that we all ended up in the same facility/care home. I was intrigued when I found out one of my fellow residents was actually one of the founders of 'the silent disco' before his accident! Bizarrely I was also astonished to find out that the new resident in my Southend care home came from the same care home in Sawbridgeworth. We were just there at different times. However, we did know several of the same people. I enjoyed following other residents' progress while living in a care home. Like one resident, I could see him finding his voice, starting walking and eventually going home. He was lucky enough to move back home. Sadly, moving back to my family home is not a viable option. This is disappointing, but, realistically would not be sustainable or beneficial for my family and me. Therefore, staying in a residential care home means receiving all my medical and care needs without placing unnecessary stress on my mum. Allowing my parents to maintain the role/relationship of my' parents', as opposed to my 'carers'.

My friends travelled from Essex to Oxford when I had my accident to come and see me. They have since maintained a prominent role in my life. I have been fortunate with my friends throughout my life. I feel highly overwhelmed that they have stayed in contact and given me continued support throughout my journey.

Each year, on the anniversary of my fall, I treat myself to celebrating life and how far I have come. I also reflect on my achievements and those that have helped me reach every milestone. I fail to find the right words to express how thankful I am. I feel 'thank you' is an understatement for all the generosity, time, kindness, love and support I have been shown by family, friends and even strangers.

Thank you would never be enough.

Nineteen

Reflection

I was always relatively modest as a child. I would avoid being the centre of attention and being in front of the camera. I would become easily embarrassed when it came to school awards. I didn't like to be the main focus. James helped me first discover who I was and find self-confidence. James made me understand the danger of joining the army and ultimately helped me change my career goal. James was near fluent enough in Spanish, whereas I had decent conversational Spanish, from being brought up around the Spanish language as my mother's side of the family originated from Gibraltar.

James used to say I was his Poquita Estrella which means a little star. I was devastated when he passed, and I had it tattooed on my wrist as a constant reminder. When I was with Neil, he disliked my tattoo so much that I went through a phase of using foundation and concealer to cover it. I even considered having a complete cover-up. I would blame marking on the bed sheet for covering the tattoo down to a bad fake tan, and I started to enquire about laser removal. I was often asked if James had not died, would I have been with him. I always found it somewhat difficult to explain no because James and I, although very similar, were also polar opposites. I was not from a financially privileged background. His dad disapproved of my opinionated ways and thought I was a bad influence and a distraction. So as far as I was concerned, James could only be my best friend.

When I met Neil on holiday, it was a complete coincidence. I was not by any means looking to meet someone at that moment. I was on a friend-only holiday and ended up meeting him randomly. He made me feel alive again, and we would alternate visits when we returned home after our holiday. At uni, I went to Oxford every weekend until I graduated, after which I decided to move there permanently. As the years rolled by, our friends started to get engaged. I thought naturally, with time, Neil and I would too marry, even though he said he never wanted to get married or have children. My dermatologist told me that if I were to have children, they would more than likely suffer from melanoma. I told Neil I had made a conscious decision that I did not want to have children knowing they would have a form of skin cancer. He said that was fine, and he didn't care. He still loved me and didn't want kids anyway.

After my accident and I had time to emerge from a coma, I have vivid memories of laying in my hospital bed looking around the bay. I recall feeling very disorientated and confused about where I was and what had happened. I remember wishing my mum or Neil would come and make everything make sense. As time progressed and I made steps in my recovery, I was transferred to a care home. I had an overwhelming feeling of guilt. I told Neil I felt as though I was holding him back. After all, I had that accident, not him, so why should he suffer. Neil took me in his arms and told me he did not care that I was disabled, loved me for me, and never wanted children anyway. However, it was only recently that he finally admitted that he had moved on with another girl. I genuinely hold no animosity for the fact that he had moved on, but I was beyond frustrated and hurt that he had lied about it for over a year. My accident has left me really emotionally fragile. Only at times of reflection can I identify all the mistakes I made in life and what I could/would've done alternatively.

I can also recognise all of my achievements. It's astonishing when I compare the initial outcome the doctor gave my family compared to everything I can do today. I mainly thank my parents for never giving up on me. Without their sacrifice, patience and determination, I would not be where I am today. My friends have been an extension of my family. They have supported me and continue sharing memories the same as before. I have realised that it is what it is in life today. Although it was not how I had planned, it's still full of love from family & friends. I need to concentrate on the new path and goals in my current life. I need to close the book on my old life, cherish memories of the good times, focus on what is awaiting ahead, and not focus on what could've been...

it's time for a
new chapter

Twenty

The Beauty Of Hindsight

Ever since the accident, I spend nearly every day thinking about how, through hindsight, I can identify all the decisions I have made throughout life. I think about those I could/would have changed, which in turn would/could have prevented my accident.

I often wonder if I had taken either opportunity to go to America, my accident would not have happened because I went. I probably would not have returned to the UK, and my relationship with Neil would not have managed to last. However, I still believe that rejecting both offers was the right decision.

My favourite and best memories involved Neil from nights out and events on holiday to boring times watching 'Breaking Bad', playing cards and the game of life. If my accident had happened in the US, I would not have received the same medical treatment. Although I would have medical insurance, it would have only covered a small portion of my treatment. It would have more than likely been the financial ruin of my parents and me.

I must shut down the book of my hard life and concentrate on making the best of life as it is now. I have been advised that I should not compare my life to my friends, family or people I know. Social media is merely a platform people use to show selected, often edited pictures/snippets of their life. My life does not accurately represent my dreams, aspirations or goals. I am living a very unique and tragic story. It's not often people experience all the turbulence I have. Therefore, I have no comparable tale to which I can take inspiration or compare my journey. I have to focus on everything I have achieved and how I have defied all medical prognoses. I am a living, breathing and talking medical miracle, not to blow my own trumpet.

I am truly blessed with the love and support of my family. My friends, who have remained an extension of my family, have been equally important. I have also got to know carers personally and formed a trust in friendship, which is a silver lining of my accident. If I had never had my accident, I would never have met such great, kind and caring individuals, with whom I also found I have lots in common. A select few carers have become a great source of support throughout my journey. They often provided great emotional support and advice when I shared personal issues/concerns.

Ultimately as my dad loves to quote,

"it is what it is; get on and deal with it."

I can enjoy life milestones such as weddings, houses and babies without all the stress by being involved in my friends' journey. I get to be the fun, loving aunt who can fill the little ones with treats and then hand them back and carry on with my day. I get to shower my friends' little ones with gifts, as I would if I had my own children. My friends involved me in their journey, so I feel part of that and do not miss out.

To protect my mental health, I have to try not to think about the past and how different actions would have had a different outcome. All it does is torture myself over what could have been. I am genuinely happy and content with my life, although vastly different from how I intended things. I have to ignore my feelings of not being good enough and focus on the many positive things and people I have in my life.

Twenty-one

Cliche

Although I have a brain injury, I remain fully compos mentis (I have total mental capacity). Sometimes it's questioned whether I had this before my accident! I understand people are trying to be either sympathetic or empathetic. Still, unless you have experienced the same as me, you can never understand how and why I will feel/react in a certain way. However, certain clichés people tend to use cause me to become easily frustrated and offended; I can easily snap back. There are particular phrases which I absolutely despise and would strongly advise against using...

"Everything happens for a reason." If this were true, I would like to know why my accident occurred.

It could be worse." I am alive, so yes, it could be worse. However, I have lost everything I have ever known or worked hard for.

Although I have quoted my dad, I can't stand being told: "it is what it is." I refuse to settle. I hate being told it is not the end of the world. For me, this is/was the end of everything I have ever known.

I hate being told that the silver lining is not dealing with all the stress connected with such momentous life events as children, work and home. It is not through choice. I am just grateful for my family and friends who have involved me in their journey and made me feel included and happy. I get to enjoy the fun bits as a friend. Ultimately this has helped soften the blow of not being able to experience it on a personal level.

Twenty-two

Emotions

As a child, I was not overly emotional. I was, however, quite sensitive. My parents never hit me but just shouted. That would be enough to make me cry. I was concerned about other people's opinions and was self-conscious. I refused to wear my hearing aids due to the whispers of classmates. I would lip-read and struggle to understand but would get the gist and muddle through. I was devastated when we moved from Enfield to Shoeburyness, purely for having to start a new senior school. I dreaded the thought that everybody would already have formed friends. I was just going to be the loner new girl – "Billy no Mates."

My school uniform was totally different in London. We wore kilts with over-the-knee socks. On my first day of senior school, I rocked up in my skirt and over-the-knee socks, thinking it was normal. Needless to say, I was wrong, and I was quickly laughed at by everyone. So I pulled up my socks the highest they could go so they looked like tights and promptly made my mum buy me black trousers, to avoid having to wear a skirt altogether. Little did I know that one of the girls making fun of me would become my best friend. It was in year 9 when I phoned my mum to say I would be home late as I had rounders practice after school. She told me I had to go home immediately as she needed to discuss something very important. All the way home, I had different tragic scenarios running through my head. Why couldn't she have just told me on the phone? It must have been bad news.

Upon my arrival, I was met by an emotional mother. She sat me down and explained my grandad had unfortunately had another massive stroke and, this time, had not survived. This was the first death I had to deal with. I remember the following day being outside my science lesson when I broke down and started crying. This was the first time my friends had seen me cry. I often would get choked up but not show my full emotions and cry. I always thought crying was a sign of weakness, so I would fight back any tears.

In my first year of college, I had heard there was a hit-and-run not far from my house on the news. My friend then called me to say that the hit-and-run was one of my close, dear friends, Joanne. I then made my mum take me to Alice's sixth form school to inform her of the dreadful news.

As it was the same day as her then-boyfriend had his driving test and didn't want her to misunderstand. Joanne's passing caused a big group of her friends to meet up on several occasions to exchange memories of Jo and genuinely offer support for each other. Joanne's funeral was one of the most emotional days I had experienced. However, I was overwhelmed by the number of people attending her funeral. They were even standing outside of the chapel. It was very nice to see just how many lives she had touched.

James planned to return home for his sister's birthday the following year and asked me to go with him. He would take me home as I was already planning to go home for Joanne's first anniversary. But I had already pre-booked and paid for my train, so I refused James' kind offer. Little did I know on his journey home, he would have a head-on collision that left him in an unresponsive, vegetative state. Doctors explained there was little to no hope. There was no brain activity, which made his parents decide to turn off his life support. Obviously, this meant he would inevitably pass away. The following week, I actually bumped into his dad and sister while he was officially withdrawing James' enrolment from university. He cruelly said, "had you taken his initial offer to go to university in America, James would have followed." He believed this meant that he would never have had the accident. He was my first love. James had always been very romantic and thoughtful. I was surprised that shortly after Valentine's Day, I received a rose and a card from him. He had pre-ordered and sent it to my parents as he knew I would be at home for my brother's birthday. I was never able to channel stress or deal with emotional situations very well, so I had a stage of passing out and having episodes of shaking like a fit. After tests for epilepsy, I discovered I had a nodule on the brain. This would inflame when I was experiencing high levels of stress/emotion, which would then cause me to have an episode.

In March 2009, my parents decided to close the business, sell our family home and move to Gibraltar. This left me feeling very lonely. However, I understood and agreed that starting life in Gibraltar would be more beneficial for my parents.

They were not getting any younger – let's face it. And the way of life was far more relaxed and slower-paced than the rat race in England. They also had lots of family members already in Gibraltar. I was already used to travelling to Gibraltar several times throughout the year to see my family. I already had pre-arranged a trip in November 2010.

However, upon arrival, it was clear this would not be like any other visit.

I collected my baggage and departed the airport, where my parents met me and drove me to my grandparents flat. They were staying there temporarily before making any decisions on investing in purchasing a property of their own. In the car park, I was told that my Grandad's aneurysm had burst the night before. There was nothing they could do, and he had passed away. My world shattered to pieces. I had only spoken to him on the phone the night before when we had no idea of the tragic events that were about to unfold. As Gibraltar is a hot country, they prefer to bury people who have died quickly. I didn't pack anything suitable for a funeral, so I had to go shopping to find something more appropriate. It was here, at the funeral, my parents found out that I smoked cigarettes.

I was so overwhelmed by the funeral and how impersonal it was that I had one of my episodes. My dad told me he knew I smoked and said I should have one to 'sort myself out.' I am so glad my mum was in Gibraltar when all this happened, as she could emotionally support my grandmother. It became apparent that living in Gibraltar was not for my parents. So they returned to England in March 2011. They started renting a house while setting up a new business. It gave them a base, and they knew the area well. It also gave me a base to visit away from my university.

I would generally cry through frustration rather than sadness.

In 2014, when I had my accident, it left me unable to channel or express my emotions. Since my accident, I have only cried on a few occasions. Once when I was scrolling through photos on my hard drive. Other times were when I found out my beloved dogs Jimmy and Bella had been put to sleep; finally, when watching the wedding video of my one-to-one carer. I was overwhelmed with how beautiful it was and the fact I would never get to have a video like that of my own. I am gutted that I will never get to walk down the aisle with my dad or make my parents into grandparents. They did such a fantastic job with my brother and me. They would have made the most perfect, loving grandparents. I am just glad to have such good friends who can share their journey of buying houses, getting married and starting families with me. I feel included. It softens the blow. I can't stand it when I'm told "never say never" because I know I am disabled. I won't miraculously wake up tomorrow or any other day and be 'normal'. Even if I could have children, I wouldn't because it is impractical, as I can't provide care for them myself. It would be morally irresponsible to have a child knowing my situation. My mum has said to me on many occasions that she does not mind not being a grandma. I have plenty of cousins that will keep her on her toes, but I know deep down she is upset, and she's just saying this, so I don't feel bad. My parents are the best aunt and uncle a kid could have, plus I am there to give suggestions for Birthday and Christmas presents. They don't ever fall into the category of lame, boring relatives.

Emotions Continued...

Before my accident, I always found humour in other people's misfortune, although never maliciously. I enjoyed watching "You've been framed," hence why the YouTube hit "Charlie bit my finger" made me laugh for the first time after emerging from my coma.

I had always used laughter to hide if I was nervous about my lack of self-confidence. This also had a negative effect, though, as I often laugh at the most inappropriate of times which can come across as rude or heartless.

I often pause to process the information I am given to provide a positive response. Still, I almost always become nervous and giggle, which can be perceived as insensitive and rude. I can assure you that I, by no means, mean to offend, be cold or harsh. I sincerely apologise if I have ever come across negatively, as this was never my intention.

I have most recently found watching 'the soaps' challenging as the storyline is centred around the character who sustained a head injury and died. Although the causes differed from mine, the resulting injuries were similar. It was most distressing to see the alternative ending. It did, however, put into perspective just how lucky I am. Although I have lost many things, I must remain grateful and persistent. Only through hard work and persistence will I improve my quality of life.

In the lead-up to Jadey's wedding, I watched countless episodes of "Say Yes To The Dress" and "Don't Tell The Bride". I always enjoyed seeing the wedding dresses. When she told me she was expecting a baby, I swapped it to "One Born Every Minute". It was nice seeing the individual stories of each person. I found the father's reactions most entertaining. Some of them were bigger girls than the women in labour!. I used to get teary at the thought that I would never be able to have my own baby. Now I focus more on that I will never have to suffer the pain of pushing essentially another human out of myself, and then the sadness just melts away.

I remind myself of my young cousins and the children my friends have and are going to have, and how I enjoy them and give them little treats as I can't spoil the kids I don't have. At least I don't have to deal with crying babies, bath time or telling an upset child "no". I get to spoil them and then give them back. I have been called every name imaginable, but 'wife' or 'mum' will never be one unless it is said in sarcasm.

Twenty-three

Acceptance

It has taken me several years to accept my accident and the changes and impact that it has had on my life. There have been several stages of acceptance.

In 2012, my oncologist explained that I would pass on the defective gene that gave me melanoma if I had children. This made me conscious not to have children because I didn't want to pass on my melanoma complications. This was not a problem for Neil as he didn't want children anyway. Therefore, I had already dealt with the emotional torment of not having children before my fall.

It wasn't until 2018 that I had eight 1 hour sessions of counselling which gave me the tools to convert negative thoughts, break them down, dissect them and then transform and reshape them. I had a short stage of deep depression, where I was given anti-depressant medication. It was a bizarre and awkward part of my life.

For as long as I can remember, my parents taught me to treat people with dignity and respect and how I want them to treat me myself. When I met Neil, I thought it must have been fate as the circumstances of how we met were too coincidental. As time progressed and our relationship progressed, I thought we would have beaten the odds and had the fairytale ending, including marriage and, eventually, a family.

My accident honestly threw a spanner in the works. He tried to be supportive by repeatedly telling me that he didn't care that I was disabled and that he would love me for me. However, this clearly was not the case. He finally admitted to me that he had, in fact, had another relationship, and they were serious enough to buy a puppy together! Then he said they had broken up, and she took the dog with her as she signed the papers when they were collecting the puppy, so she was technically the owner. At this point, I blocked Neil on all social media, including Whatsapp, and I have not spoken to him since. I don't have any desire to maintain any form of contact with him. It is only now that I truly understand how you can "love someone" without being in love with them. I don't have any animosity toward him, but I will never forgive him for how he treated me.

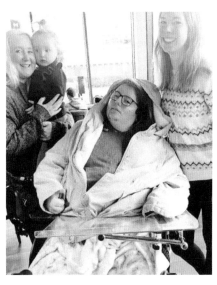

I feel fortunate and blessed that I have such fantastic family and friends. They have continuously included me on their journey of marriage and having children. It breaks my heart that I will never walk down the aisle with my dad and will never be able to have children. Still, I have accepted that my body is merely a shell. My personality and heart remain the same as before my accident. I now get the pleasure of spoiling the little ones without dealing with the tantrums.

Every day, I look at the canvas my mum gave me at Christmas. That, and the plaque from my auntie Dianne is a constant reminder that even the slightest wishes do come true and that I should never give up or stop striving for more.

I have joined several online communities and groups where I can interact with other TBI survivors. I can express and compare feelings and experiences and exchange advice on treatments and medicines that others have had. I was scrolling through TikTok one day when I came across Liam, a gentleman who ran the impact London community. It focuses on mental health and well-being. I felt normal by having everyday conversations about simple things, like, Love Island. He took the time to learn and understand my story and gave me time and help to take part in group discussions.

Twenty-four

Adapting and Adjusting

Before my accident, my knowledge of the care system was somewhat basic. It was minimal as I had never had any experience in it besides the small pieces I picked up from my granddad. Since 2014, I have found myself being an actual part of the "system." It was only then that I understood the role/ responsibility of being a carer.

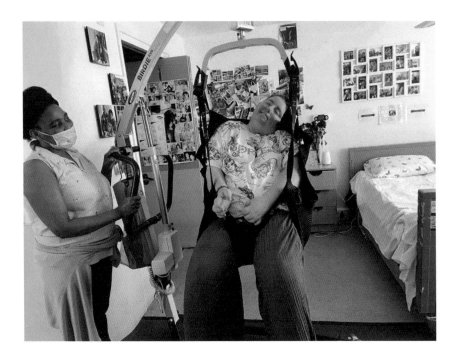

Unfortunately, we were not in a position where we could adapt our family home, even if we were given the opportunity. I would not be happy because it would not be just physically adapting the property for my wheelchair and equipment. It would also have drastically changed the family home's whole dynamic. My brother and I have not lived at home for several years. Therefore, my Mum and Dad had adapted to living as just the two of them with the dog.

I would have had to have had community carers several times throughout the day to provide me with personal care. Residing in a care home surrounds me with other disabled people and dedicated staff, allowing me to maintain a parent-child relationship. My parents are not restricted with the frequency of their visits from care staff, so they have sustained a separate role. It means I must be more proactive and forward-thinking in planning activities with my parents.

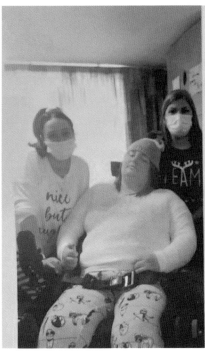

After my accident, we sold my car when it became clear that I would no longer have the requirement to drive. We purchased a wheelchair-adapted vehicle which my parents could drive. We have additional passenger space to allow room for my one-to-one carer. We have BlueTooth available for the radio, so I was more than happy.

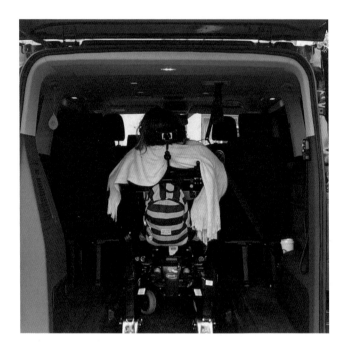

Obviously, being in such close and intense contact with the care staff and one-to-one support, I have naturally formed a powerful bond with them. They know all of my past, and I managed to build such trust, allowing me to express any emotion I felt. They have encouraged me with my speech and have discovered alternative solutions to everyday tasks, e.g. drinking. We found it easy to drink from a drinking cup and lid similar to that in Starbucks! I have since purchased a personalised cup.

After my accident, I had to consciously try not to compare my life with others. I had not met anyone who has been through a similar experience, so I have nothing to compare my life to. I cannot compare myself to other people my age as I will never have the same milestones. Instead, my friends involve me in their achievements and events in their lives, like buying a house, getting married and having children.

When all the drama unfolded regarding Neil, I decided to block him and everyone who was a former mutual friend. I deleted anybody I had not been in contact with for over a month. I now see my past as life lessons which have made me stronger and wiser.

I now have firmly closed the door on how my life used to be

and look forward to creating new memories with the loved ones that have stuck around and the incredible people I have met along the way.

At the care home in Sawbridgeworth, we went to a local icerink. To my surprise, they placed my wheelchair on the ice. This was an excellent activity as I could do something I had done many times before. I was able to take part. I wasn't made to sit on the side and watch.

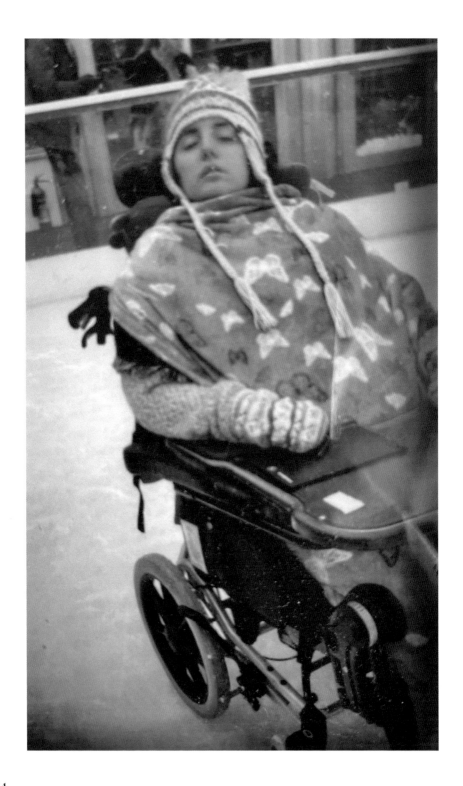

I was incredibly fortunate to go to Gibraltar with my family. To my surprise, they had the most mind-blowing equipment on the actual beach⊠ a hoist and a floating buggy, allowing me to go into the sea. It was bloody colder than I remembered, but it made me feel normal again.

I have also been countless times, to the cinema, which has a dedicated place for wheelchair users. I have also been bowling, playing with the bumpers on and using the ramp to roll the ball down!

I am still adventurous and open to other activities for disabled wheelchair users. There was talk of assisted skiing, which I feel very excited about!

After my accident, I was restricted to bed washes and the odd shower. Initially, with a shower trolley, but when I moved homes, I was finally given the pleasure of having a bath! They have an adapted bath, and I have 1 bath a week. I take full advantage of the opportunity to use bubble bath, bath bombs, facemasks, and all my lotions and potions. Plus, I have my music.

After all. I have years worth of baths to make up for. don't I?

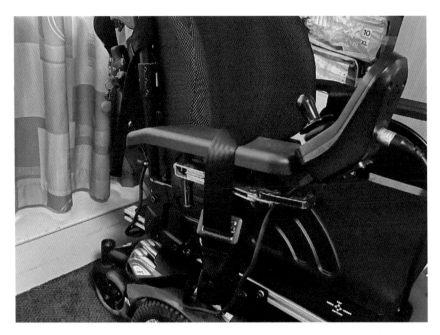